When Life is Lovable
and
Love is Livable

and
Other Stories

by
Adnan Sarhan

ADNAN SARHAN, director of the Sufi Foundation of America is a master of various traditions of scholarship, meditative sciences, physical exercise, mystical dance and music. He is internationally known for his "Rapid Method" which develops higher intelligence and awareness, and which causes people to become creative and innovative by destroying all types of bad habits.

Adnan leads participants in a wide range of timeless techniques. The work signals a connection to the past which stretches back twelve hundred years. Exercises, meditation, drumming, movement, dancing and whirling are used to heighten concentration and produce bodily changes, including slower heart rates, lower blood pressure, and shifts in perception opposite to those caused by stress.

Over the years Adnan has conducted workshops at prestigious institutions throughout the United States and many other countries of the world. Each summer he directs an intensive two-month seminar at the Sufi Foundation Retreat Center in the Manzano Mountains of New Mexico. For further information about that program, contact: Sufi Foundation, P.O. Box 170, Torreon, NM 87061, (505) 384-5135, www.sufifoundation.org.

Table of Contents

People of the Mirage and Other Stories

When Life is Lovable
and
Love is Livable

When Life is Lovable and
Love is Livable

Eat Hershey and you will be marshy. Eat Twinkies and you will be kinky. Drink whiskey and you will be a monkey. And your negative thoughts become the block to knowing your thoughts. Your negative thoughts tie your nervous system in knots and shrink your spirit just like a woolen shirt or pants when washed in hot water. The sleeves become half sleeves and the pants become short pants half-way below the knees.

And you're planning to go to a dress-up party. You are in a hurry. And there is nothing else to wear. And you go anyway. And automatically people think of you as a short-sleeved person without using their minds. Because sometimes seeing prevents thinking -- and that is the real seeing when you are aware. So why waste a thought when the short sleeve is a short sleeve. For you to remedy the situation, eat strawberry shortcake to be even.

Your Life as a Frozen Cabbage

Actually a short brain wave comes from a short-circuit in the nervous system. And as a result of that, the spirit becomes like a frozen cabbage in a box of ice in a giant supermarket. And when the spirit becomes a frozen cabbage you will be walking down the aisle dragging your legs as if they were frozen. And your eyes glaze on the signs that are hanging from the ceiling to show what kind of products are on the shelves. And your body is numb and your brain is going hodge-podge. And no wonder, you are looking at these signs as if you are looking at the Seven Wonders of the World.

And you mumble when you are close to the bread section, "Oh, my gosh! I smell fresh, hot Wonder Bread! It looks as if it just came out of the oven. Wouldn't it be great to have a snack before supper of a Wonder Bread sandwich with peanut butter, jelly, marmalade, a lot of butter with a few chocolate chip cookies inside of it, and dip it in maple syrup till it looks like a saturated sponge in a sink filled with water after washing the dishes. Oh boy! I can't resist it. So I'm going to do it now. And eat it with a bottle of 16 oz. Pepsi. And I will sit in a grocery at the table next to the water fountain, so I can quench my thirst if I have to."

Lingering in the Pepsi Time

"I have developed the habit of drinking water with the Pepsi to dilute it and to enjoy lingering in the Pepsi time. And then black coffee with sugar and apple pie with ice cream. It will be an excellent appetizer for the evening meal. I am trying to feast tonight on a whole barbecued pig. How beautiful and how dreamy life is when you eat baby barbecued pig! I love it. I enjoy it. And I wish to live forever, to keep munching, chewing, eating from the fat of the land and from the fat of the belly of the pig. And I have one request to ask God and that is to increase the population of the pigs more than rabbits, horses, goats, sheep and cows because it is my favorite food. Pig is number one!

"And I hate to eat goat. And I don't care for beef because of all the hormones and chemicals that they give them to eat, that are positively not only hazardous to health but dangerous to eat. All the people who eat beef have a heavy beefy look on their appearance. I have made a vow never to touch or taste beef. And if people keep eating beef with hormones and chemicals it will cause damage to the brain and absolutely disintegrate the spirit as if it had never been created. And sooner or later they will lose their capacity to talk. Instead of talking, they'll be mooing like a cow.

"Imagine sitting in a steak house where all the people are mooing and all the waitresses are mooing back to them. So, my friend, I give you the most precious advice and do it now. That is, stop eating beef before mooing."

Neither Animal Nor Human

When your spirit is a frozen cabbage you will be a creature neither animal nor human being. Your negative thought not only alienates you from the people but from yourself as well. You are a stranger to the people and to yourself. And the people are strangers to you and to themselves because you and the people are in the same boat drifting in a sea of tribulation, heavy fog with no shore in sight, confused, hopeless, lost in a sea of fallible, corrupted ways of existence based on weak, wicked technology and material that keep the people constantly in a state of anxiety and tension till the day they finish their lives, with a song on their lips that goes:

Bye, bye, chocolate
Bye, bye, wine
Hello, loneliness
I think I am going to die.

But you should not worry about "going to die" because you have been dead since you were born in this materialistic system of refutable and dead products that only have appeal and glamour to the eyes of ignorant and spiritless people. Form gravitates towards form. And the animal self within has no limit or contentment in acquiring and having anything that it gets a

9

hold on. The more you acquire, the more the lust blossoms out of proportion and hits you with a bombardment of anxiety, tension, confusion, jitteriness, and makes you look like a heinous creature. And whenever you sleep and wake and move, or wherever you go, you are enclosed in a cocoon of disturbance and hideous anxiety. You are the center of a pool of radiation of negative vibrations that anyone with common sense, if they have common sense, would run away just like a rabbit running for his life from a wolf.

The Joy of Material

When you are bound to the junk of the material and you put the material above you and you become in subordination to the material, then you are in complete ignorance to what is the purpose of the material.

The fact is, God created you and God created the material for your grandeur and elevation and gave you the spirit, and that is part of His Essence, to command and rule with justice, peace, understanding and love. But when you let the material rule and control you, you become a slave to the material.

The material has no passion, no love, no imagination. The material is a tough, vicious slave master with no compassion. And voluntarily you enslave yourself to the cog and wheel in the factory. And you lose the value of your identity and yourself. You lose the value of man and humanity. The world becomes, in your eyes, grim yellow, and the light of the sun becomes a dim, gray and muddy color without enthusiasm, without life, and without rejuvenation and without the beat of the heart, while the sky is a delightful turquoise and when a pure cool breeze caresses your face and makes your senses quiver

10

as if you were meeting your beloved that you are amorously in love with.

You complain. You are negative. You have no rest. And if you have time to rest, you spend it in bars to drink and bring numbness to your brain. And this is another kind of slavery.

There are limitless ways of being a slave to different objects. Each habit you have will multiply your state in slavery. And the habits thrive in a materialistic system where consciousness and spirit are absent. And because you are enslaved to all these dumb and stupid masters, you must be more dumb and stupid than they are.

You deserve to inhale smog, and to smoke and destroy your lungs, and to drink liquor and destroy your brain, and to be nervous, to have no rest and to be anxious without harmony, and to be angry without peace and suspicious without tranquility of the mind, and to be in a depression without happiness of the heart, and to be sullen without the joy of a smile, and to be dim-eyed without the shining spirit. So you deserve all of that because it is your choice.

Why Be a Slave If You Could Be Free

And the Koran said, "Man is born free." But with the freedom he is given a choice. And the choice is either positive or negative. Whatever you follow, it will be the eventual consequence of your choice. And your life either will be felicity and joy or, if you take the negative choice, your life will be suffering and misery.

11

When you are attached to the material that is dead, because you are dead, then you will lose your humanity. You will never know the meaning of man or how lovable, beautiful, perfect and suave man is when the spirit is alive within him.

When Material Is Alive

If the spirit is alive in a man the material becomes alive too. The material becomes like a mirror and reflects back to you joy and pleasure. And the material becomes beautiful. It will be complimentary to the spirit. It enhances it and makes life gentle, harmonious, tender and joyful.

When the spirit is alive and awake you could look at a stone and you will see an energy that comes out of the stone that vibrates with harmony and peace. And you will feel a communication of subtle and deep radiation. You become attuned to it. You will feel contentment and relaxation that is unknown in the ordinary way. Every cell in your body and brain becomes exaggerated with a unique joy and a healing process overwhelms you.

You become in the moment. And the world stops to talk to you. And you will be showered with the peace that is hidden inside eternity. And the eternity will lift its veil and you become face to face with truth and reality. And whatever exists in the world of suffering and strife, anxiety and tension will disappear as though it never existed. And you will see the eternal love that is unknown by the people who only chase their tails.

What I said is a fact that can be obtained by anyone. But they have to work toward it to earn it. It is very possible but not for people who make themselves dumb and stupid, on and on, every day of their lives by doing every wrong thing and thinking they are doing right. Weakness, sickness, confusion, tension, anger, sleeping with sadness and waking up with fear, pollution of the brain, the body and the environment are all but little examples that you are doing wrong.

The Little Basement Under The Bottom of The Sea

You can tell a little creature crawling on the bottom of the sea that there is a sun in the sky and that it is outside of the sea. And there is a big, big empty space and there is no water in it except rain sometimes to make things green and beautiful. And the little crawling creature, Kar-Kootch el Moo-Kar-Ketch brought his head out of the basement that he dug under the floor of the sea and he said, "You are either joking or brainless. There is no such thing as a sun in the sky in an empty space. But what is a sun? And what do you mean by a sun? I've never heard of it.

"And my grandfather and grandmother heave never heard of it. Besides that, my grandfather was known as the greatest savant, philosopher, thinker and compiler of the old scriptures that all the fish, the creatures and the chicken of the sea read and followed in their life in everything, even to regulate their diet and how much salt water they were to drink for health reasons and ecology of the environment. And I used to remember my grandfather saying, 'Coke is absolutely forbidden to fish, otherwise they will pollute their blood and their tails will lose the graceful kick and wiggle. And they will lose their speculation and awareness.'

"So the sun does not exist. And a rain that makes things beautiful and green -- what a nonsense thing! What could be

13

more beautiful than water on water on water, above you, under you and on the four corners of the sea. And where are the four corners of the sea? No one ever will know. And also the water on water on water has no end. And it is flavored with salt. So what could a man desire more than that?

"So it is better for you to be straight and go to work in the chicken-of-the-sea factory. Get the bones and color them red, pink, blue or any other color. Then sell them in a big department store downtown. And when the fish have their lunch hour break in the mid-day, after work, they will be shopping and will buy your products for decoration. And you will be a productive, useful member of the community."

The States of Light and Dark

In life there are two states that exist. One is the state of darkness where even if you are under the bright light of the sun, the inside of you is dark. The other is the state of light where even if you are in the darkest of night, the inside of you is light.

When people are in the state of darkness they usually do not know that they are in the state of darkness. And what makes them not capable of seeing where they are is the ignorance of the self. I will give you some clues about how to know if you are in the state of darkness. These are when you are negative, tense, unhappy, bored, feeling monotonous, tired of where you are at, anxious, disturbed, with fluctuation in the thought, nervous, sad, greedy, possessive, rigid, with no flexibility, argumentative, obnoxious, a bore to yourself and others, always in conflict with yourself and others, a pessimist, weak, unmannered, gruff, a miser, penny-pincher, never knowing the meaning of generosity, unhelpful, selfish, egotistical, finding fault even in an angel; a victim of habits whether drugs or liquor, coffee, coke and all the useless soft drinks, cigarettes, marijuana, hash, heroin, cocaine, crack, snuff, tobacco chewing, abusive ways of eating, chocolate, cake, pastries and all the junk food; a victim of your senses and sensuality, never smiling, sinking eyes with sadness, thrashing with anger, rough and never knowing how to be suave, crude, rude, cumbersome, odious, melancholy, and mortified. These are just some of the clues. But there are many others that contribute to your state of misery and disastrous existence till you die. And you will never know the meaning of excellence or contentment.

The other state, and that is the state of light, as I said before, even in the darkest of night, you are light inside. You will be in the state of light if you have peace, faith and excellence (in Arabic: *Islam*, *Iman*, and *Ihsan*). When these three elements are acquired by any person, he will be perfect. And *El ihsan el kamel* in Arabic means the complete or perfect human being.

Peace

When you are in the state of peace, you will be in good relation with the space. And that is the empty space. And you might think of it as an empty space, but it is the most meaningful element in the universe, in the existence, and the life of creation. And it is because of the space that you are able and capable of seeing and witnessing the most miraculous things in the existence, and the most profound, exhilarating, magical phenomena of wonder that are in the space.

You are able to see the sun, the moon, the stars, the clouds, the blue sky, the distance, the mountains, the valleys, the trees, the plants, the birds that fly and sing, riding on the

15

breeze, and the butterfly gliding in the air, drifting, dancing and singing, and the leaves of the trees quivering playfully, glistening in the light of the sun, applauding to the song of the wind, telling the wind, "Come and embrace us. We love the coolness in you. It invigorates our spirit and makes our cheeks red and makes us dance with you in the biggest ballroom that is in the lap of nature, in the valleys of dreams and in the mountains of romance." And in the space you could fly a kite. And in the space you could enjoy watching the sparrows flying, singing, twisting and wiggling their tails. And peace fills the heart of those with good intentions.

Faith

Faith -- that is a very beautiful word. The Arabic word is *Iman*. Some of the meanings of this word in Arabic are: security, trust, ease, peaceful existence, creativity, positive thinking, acceptance, reflection of delight, happiness and contentment. And because of the varied meanings of the word, *Iman*, and that is faith, you find yourself pulled in all these positive aspects. And naturally your faith becomes strong like a solid stone, unshakable. And the word faith grows and gives you protection like a shield. And then you will have faith in life. And the life becomes faithful to you. You have to have faith in your life. In reality, there is no choice about it because if you have faith in your life you will recognize it, respect it, and honor your life. If you honor your life, the existence and the universe will honor you.

If you have no faith in your life, you will be miserable, confused, and the existence and the universe will look down on you and abandon you. And you will be filled with doubt, confusion and fear. And your life will be nothing but suffering.

If you do any kind of work and you have faith in it, the work will grow and you will be happy. If you have no faith in your work, the work will diminish and you will be sorrowful. If you are writing a letter with faith, it will be a beautiful letter. Without faith, it will be bothersome. If you drink a glass of water with faith, it will give you a healing power. Without faith you will complain about the water and will drink coke instead. And each time you drink coke it will reduce your vigor and health one degree lower.

In everything in life, you have to have faith. Faith is a precious gift from heaven and it is a trustworthy object. If you accept it and trust in it, your life will be beautiful and contentment will promote your action. You will never need to go to psychologists, counselors or therapists. You will be your own psychologist, counselor or therapist. And with discernment and awareness of the heart, you will solve any problem or there will be no problems. Discernment and awareness are a natural process and product of peace and faith. When you have peace, there is no room for problems. Problems exist only when there is no peace.

Excellence

Also in the state of light, the highest aspect that is most valuable is *El Ihsan* and that is excellence. In whatever you do seek excellence. If you seek excellence, you become excellent. And Mohammed said, "God loves those who do a work and perfect it." Also he said, "Work with one thing at a time and God will take care of the rest." Also he said, "Work with the easy things and the difficult things become easy." And also he said, "Work for your life as if you live forever and work for your later days as if you die tomorrow." That saying combines the mundane and the spirit and molds them in oneness without separation.

To be responsible, to seek perfection in your life and not to neglect the spirit, and by molding them together, the life becomes the spirit and the spirit becomes life. That is the most perfect and the highest thing in the existence. That is the state of excellence, where the light opens to it and the state of light brings *ma'arifa*. It means knowledge of the self and the universe that is in the heart.

So if you are sweeping the floor and to create a faith in the sweeping tell yourself, "I am going to do it very well and I will make the floor excellent." And excellence could start as simply as sweeping the floor and it goes as high as knowing God. All the work that is done whether sweeping, washing dishes, washing clothes, fixing sidewalks, working with flowers, taking care of a garden, painting a wall, cleaning a kitchen or any other kind of work, when it is done with faith, it becomes an allegory for a deeper meaning in the spirit. And the connection between the two is the *humma* which means spiritual yearning that is vitalized by action when the faith is directing it. Ibn Ata'illah said, "Deeds or work are forms that exist, their spirit is the secret loyalty in them."

The Peach from Mozambique

The closed mentality of the people who are lost in the wonder of material causes them to miss the simplicity of life and the beauty of nature. The taste of the ripe peach hanging on a tree, juicy, red, nectar-dripping when its skin bursts open from the impact of the ripeness... and the sweetness and the taste of the unripe peach that is canned in Mozambique and forgotten in a dingy little basement store in the East End of London for three years... are alike to the people who have lost the taste in their tongues, because of eating too many chemicals and poison that come in many forms, like chocolate

18

wrapped in beautiful, colorful paper, pastries made with tons of sugar and so on and on.

Eating a peach that comes in a can with water and sugar and added chemicals to preserve it is not like eating a peach from a tree laden heavily with peaches that are ripe, juicy, orange in color with red make-up on their cheeks, playing with the wind, sparkling in the sun, filling the space with joy and the eyes with delight like a living, crackling red flame in a cottage on a mountain on a cold night when the snow is all white.

And those beautiful peaches are gently swinging and swaying, dancing and playing on their branches heavily filled with sweet juice like honey. And from the ripeness and sweetness they feel as if they are jumping out of their skins and become cautious of falling on the ground.

The Breeze and His Love for The Perfumed Peach

And the breeze says to them, "Don't worry. You will not fall on the ground because I love you. I will take care of you. I will embrace you and will not let you fall. I love to watch you dance in the space and to see the blue sky smiling on your red cheeks. And I smell your perfumed sweet cheeks that make me elated and fill me with joy and tranquility. I will dance with you and blow on the leaves. They will make music and I will sing with them. And you will dance for me. And I will dance for you. I am the spirit and you are the form. And when the spirit and form dance together they will create life, love and beauty. The existence and creation become vibrant and vibrate with sensuality, passion and spirit."

And the peach says to the breeze, "Thank you for not letting me fall. I love it when you hold me gently. The sensuality of the form and its tender movement, the passion of the soul and its emotion, the spirit of the heart -- and when the intelligence becomes its heart, then knowing becomes intuition and discernment becomes the adornment of life and the life becomes meaningful and the life fulfills its destiny as best as it could."

And *El Tawhiid* -- unity is when the inner of you and the inner of the cosmos manifest themselves to each other and become a natural creed, so easy, so beautiful to obtain, just as if you are sitting under a peach tree and you hear a voice above you. You look up and you will see the most gorgeous, ripe, juicy peach laden with sweet honey.

And the peach says, "Hi, there. What are you doing down there? Come and get me. I am ripe. I am beautiful. I am a delight. I am sweet and I am honey. And if you don't come I will fall in you lap because my destiny is complete. You could eat me and I will give you vitality, strength, and power with joy and delight."

The Glow, the Spark and the Fire of Life

The glow, the spark and the fire of life at its best exists in the present. And the present exists in the moment where life is pure, beautiful, delightful and contented. And the time and space become like heaven, or the heaven comes to them and fills them with tranquility, intelligence of the heart and the extract of life unknown to the rational, intel-lectual mind. And the heart, the space and the time fly in each others arms like drops of water when they mix and become all water -- no separation, no division and no conflict is left.

The glow, the spark and the fire of life is at its worst when your thought is in the future or the past and when the present drifts in front of your eyes and you are unaware of it. How amazing and baffling it is to see a man who is created with the best constitution and is given intelligence with which nothing in the entire existence can compare! No money, no wealth, no gold, no treasure and none of the junk and material could do any good without the miraculous intelligence. This miraculous intelligence is the root, the foundation and the base of life when life is lovable, and love, when love is livable. And the richness of the intelligence, and that is the intelligence of the heart, is beyond what man could conceive of as the meaning of "richness."

The Tranquility of Beer

But when the intelligence of the heart is blank and obliterated and man turns to the intellect of the mind, the wheels of the intellect in the head keep going like in a factory that requires calculation. And the man sees great profit in hanging billboards to glorify beer and the tranquility of the beer, its fun, play and joy -- without realizing that this kind of tranquility, fun, play and joy will fill him with poison and make him disturbed, and positively will result in a certain damage to certain compartments in the brain that will cause great physical difficulty, and even the smile becomes strained. And smiling becomes the hardest chore to do.

This is just one of the abuses that man will indulge in when he operates from the head only, without the spirit. But man should know that liquor and drugs, like cocaine and so on, are assuredly the ways to ruin and dissolution. And there is no escape from disaster and dissolution. And the blessing never comes near people who are heedless, who have no respect for the existence, for the cosmos, or even for themselves. And Ghazalli said, "The ignorant plunge into sensual pleasures with the avidity of brutes."

The Gloom of the Dark Forces

And the Koran said, "God sends *el rijjz* to those who are heedless." The meaning of *el rijjz* is a murky, dirty, filthy state of being. Within it is confusion, worriness, doubt, misery, tiredness, ugliness, unpleasantness, disrespect, greed, selfishness, blankness, negative thought, suspicion, frozen countenance, dead eyes, mummified smile and sullen face that gives you the creeps, that the face of the devil is more pleasant and more harmonious to look at. The heedless state supports the ignorant state and the ignorant state supports the heedless state. And the ego is the link between the two. And selfishness becomes the color of the person. And on the face of that person you will see black flashes that say: selfish, greedy, and unhappy person. And those flashes flash every moment, day and night, awake or asleep till the end of life.

Intelligence and the Beautiful Life

In this world there are two distinct ways of life: one is the beautiful and the other is the ugly. The beautiful life is possible if you look to your intelligence with awe and respect and value it as the most valuable treasure in the entire existence. Intelligence is the crown of life, love and the inner pleasure of the heart. Intelligence is pure joy and delight. Intelligence is breath and breath is intelligence. When they are united, the heaven and earth become one within you. Intelligence is life and life is intelligence. If you have no intelligence, you have no life, even if you are living. It doesn't matter. A donkey is living too.

Good intention brings the intelligence to a good action. And intelligence motivates good intentions. The intelligence is your guard, your shield, you protector, promoter and guide. Intelligence of the heart opens you to sensitivity, discernment, awareness, intuition, knowing, feeling, loving, getting out of life the most that there is in life. And life becomes waves of delight and sweet breath. Life becomes positive energy and reflects to you perfect harmony. You see it in the sand and the pebbles and the stones, in the dirt, in the rocks, in the mountains and the valleys, in the trees, leaves and grass, in the earth and space, in the light and all that exists. And time becomes tame.

And the tame time will sit waiting in the door of intelligence. And the time and life becomes still. The moment bursts with love and opens itself unto you. And the true reality that was hidden within the moment manifests itself to wonder after wonder. And the domain of peace becomes your lovable host. And the soul basks in the protection and warmth of the true knowledge.

And the Koran said, "You will see what no eyes have ever seen and no ears have ever heard."

The Sweet Stillness of Time

The moment becomes the essence of the eternal dance and life becomes the dance of the moment. The moment becomes the past, the present and the future. Its secret hidden depth becomes manifested like a beautiful rose, perfumed by the eternity and nurtured by the sweet stillness of time. And under the pure light of intelligence it shows itself in dazzling delight.

And the moment says, "I am the moment and I am the

23

heart of time. I am the love of the heart of time. I am still and timeless. I am so little and tiny that even the blink of an eye exceeds me and is a giant next to me. Yet I am the foundation of time and the perpetual eternity.

"I am soft like a rose in bloom. I am tender like the light of the moon. I am pure like spring water gushing and rushing to celebrate its joy and purity to meet the light of the sun, to dance in the light, with the light, for the light. And light and purity when they meet, the essence of their life becomes lovable. The life becomes love beyond love, a love that is inspired by the depth of existence, by the space when the space becomes open and takes you in. And your thought expands with the expansion of the space when you are inside it, with no limit nor end. And that entire empty space becomes a loving force of joy, delight, tranquility, harmony, and love on love on love like layers of water in the sea of perpetual, limitless space, rising and falling, singing and dancing, playing and laughing, and the waves holding, impressing, interlacing, floating with tranquility in an ease that never wanes.

"And there in clarity -- the spirit and intelligence, the soul and passion, the body and sensation; there in the love, the life and the existence, bound together in a unity, *tawhiid*, in love, *ashque*. And I am the moment in the midst of all that.

"I am the secret. I am the key, joy and love. I am in heaven and on earth. I am as easy and simple as a glass of water to a thirsty man in the desert, and could expand as big as the limitless space."

Mohammed, the master of the two worlds, the mundane world and the world of the spirit said, "Whoever lives out what he knows will receive from God what he does not know."

And the celebrated master Ibn Ata'illah said, "Actions are lifeless forms, but the presence of an inner reality of sincerity within them is what endows them with life-giving spirit."

The Opening of the Open Eyes

The apparent and the hidden are two aspects that exist in the world and the cosmos. The apparent are things that you can see. And the hidden are the things that you can't see, just like if you close your eyes and you cannot see anything. But when you open them you will see what is there to be seen. But the hidden things cannot be seen even when you open your eyes. To be able to see the hidden you need the opening of the open eyes. And to be able to open the open eyes you need to harness all your capacity, faculty, mind, body and soul toward that goal. You need to acquire force, power, strength, energy and vitality, and to keep your being intact and your intentions positive and your desire pierced deeper and deeper in the spirit, and to have no other desire but the desire for the knowledge of the self.

Any other desire will stop you short of the noblest, the finest, the highest and the best of whatever exists in life, the world, the reality and the entire cosmos. Any other desire is nothing but a waste of time and energy and will throw you out of balance from the road of roses, the spirit, the knowledge and from the grandest achievement.

While you exist in the body that has two eyes that look like projectors that you could turn them in the space and heaven as far as there is heaven and all the rest of the apparent things that you see all the time. Within that body there are magical, miraculous forces and power and capacities that recognize no limit. It is in your hand to control that body and use it to the real destiny of finding what is hidden in the inner reality of the secret existence.

If you let your body control you, you will be a loser in life. You will be like the weed in an untended garden while the perfumed roses are in heaven. The degree of how much development in the spirit you acquire depends on the degree of intensity of your desire to perceive in the spirit.

The only reason for man to exist and the only reason that man is given the intelligence is to learn about the self. Otherwise, if this were not the case, then he would be given intelligence the same as the donkey intelligence and a set of hooves and a voice to bray with for excitement and rejuvenation, and long ears that would stand erect when the braying takes place to listen to the impact and the effect of the voice on the environment and other creatures.

Shovelling Papers

When people think that they are in a hurry, busy and not having enough time to finish what they are doing, actually what they are saying is nonsense. In reality, they are doing nothing and going nowhere, even if they work twenty-four hours a day, seven days a week, the whole year, nonstop. And even if they drive thousands upon thousands of miles, or spend half or all of their lives on the highways, they are only covering distance without a connection to the distance itself because wheels run fast on paved roads.

And when you are not connected with the distance you will have the look of a glued face with invisible cement glue. And you look like a fish who lost his smile when the sea receded and left that poor fish on a bunch of dry seaweed out of his habitat. And he got habititis from smelling the smoke and the smog and there was no drop of water in sight.

When the people are in a hurry to be in their offices to do more computer work, typing, telephoning, and more paper shuffling till it comes out of their ears, they get tense and nervous. They will bite on the papers mistaking it for thin pizza especially if there is a pizza shop under the office. And the smell of the pizza climbs the space little by little and wafts quickly through the window of the office and one of the office workers shouts out "I'll take Coke with my pizza."

Also, they do typing and telephoning with coffee and smoking, getting more nervous and tense as they shovel endless papers. And moodiness becomes the mood of the day or any day.

Take your choice. But really there is no choice because the gloomy moodiness becomes ingrained in the brain that causes shrinkage in the muscles of the neck that reflect in a permanent horrible look on the face that even the wolfman, when the moon is full, if he faced that face, would turn running and screaming, "Help! Help! I saw Wolf Frankenstein!"

And the negative thought in the head makes the eyes move side to side instead of up and down. And a man in that state looks like a fat badger who is lost, not in a maze of dirt, but in a maze of useless papers. And that badger of a man thinks that these papers are useful to advance the cause of humanity and society and also to maintain his financial stature to support his habit of pie and ice cream and his real delight: JELLO -- pink, red or green -- after every meal. Especially when watching television, it is a must, the jello. And it has to be fast or a tantrum and traumatic fit will seize him from the back of his neck and force him to bend his head downward. And his voice starts to crackle like an angry rooster whose crown was chewed by a hungry rat while he was asleep, so that he had to call his therapist for help and had to go and see him immediately. And he feels worse than bad because he could not continue watching his favorite program on television: "How to Make Exclusive Divine Sweet and Mouth-Watering Pie to Increase the Delight Day and Night."

Filling the Time

Spiritless people are ignorant. When they are ignorant, they will fill the time during their work, and during their pleasure, and during the time between pleasure and work when they are bored. They fill all these times with dead time because when the heart is dead whatever you do is dead.

And the joy of life becomes really joyous when the heart is alive. But when there is no life in the heart, the life becomes gloomy, dark and morbid and morbidity becomes the normal state. A man with a dead heart indulges in his sensuality to uplift his heart. And by catering to the negative self and the ego, he sinks more and more in dark abhorrence. And the man becomes a replica of a man that looks like a man. But the inside of the man is empty and hollow without understanding of a man or of what is a man. And when the man deteriorates in his spirit, his brain becomes like hay.

And if the donkey finds that, he will want to eat it and the man will be running all over Central Park because the donkey is chasing him. And the donkey will say, "I love hay man, and hay is good to eat." And the donkey says, "A teddy bear is more pleasant to look at. And I'd rather give him a ride on my back, than a man without a brain. You could talk to a teddy bear and he will smile at you. But if you talk to a man with

28

a hay-brain, he will be blank or erupt in anger."

A dead tree in the middle of the Sahara desert in a hot summer with the temperature of 120 gives no shade, and a deadly morbid feeling surrounds it. That is exactly what a man is with a dead heart.

The Little Puppy Pum Pum Tells About the Spirit

A little puppy with a living heart and sparkling eyes, jumping and barking with enthusiasm and loving what he is doing is more honorable and blessed by God. And the little puppy, Pum Pum said, "Spirit is fun, joy, and happiness. Spirit is well-being and contentment." In that moment the little puppy, Num Num, with white sheep-like hair and black twinkling eyes with a natural wink in her right eye and a red ribbon around her neck with a bell hanging on it, she is the girlfriend of Pum Pum, jumped from behind a bush and said, "Hi, Pum Pum. I heard you talking but I see no dog to talk to. Are you talking to yourself?"

And Pum Pum said, "Be quiet, Num Num, you will never understand what I am doing. I am not talking to dogs. I am preaching to human beings. And some of them will understand what I am saying and some others will not understand."

And Num Num said, "But what are you saying?"

And Pum Pum said, "What I am saying is beyond the understanding of dogs and beyond the understanding of some human beings . . .

"If you think you are spiritual but you are tense, negative and confused, then you are in the lowest state of existence and you are a victim of illusion. If you project yourself as spiritual in your appearance, manner, behavior and conduct and your intellect commands you on how to be spiritual, be sure that the inside of you is empty and hollow. And to survive the situation eat a pink and white candy cane and wear a red bow on your neck, and that is one level of consciousness and salvation. If you want to flow and stay even with people who are flowing without knowing where they are flowing to, be aware that the spirit is nowhere near you. If you give the impression that you are spiritual, and when an event takes place and you show your selfishness and greed, that is an indication of your childish state.

"The only one true way in life is to go toward the self within. And the only way to do things or work, is to do them with the spirit. But if you do anything with the spirit and you still have a gloomy face, be sure that your work with the spirit is only imagination and speculation in your head."

And Puppy Num Num said to Puppy Pum Pum, "I love you, Pum Pum, and I love your graceful disposition and your wisdom. And most of all I love the twinkle in your eyes. They are like stars in a dreamy summer night spreading their light in heaven and falling to surround and hug the wild roses that sway in the breeze of night, drunk from the nectar of life, content in the flowers and the moment after the rain has visited them, and the flowers spread on the desert like a colorful Persian carpet. It is perfect purity that gives purity to the heart and clarity to the mind."

Puppy Pum Pum said, "Oh, Num Num, I never heard you talk like that. All you wanted to do before was to swing and eat cheese. And after swinging you wanted Coke."

Num Num said, "I know, I know, but last week I had a premonition that I wanted to change from this swinging and Coke drinking to stillness and fruitful thinking. So I was reading a New Age magazine and I discovered a whole new world of beads and colorful strings and crystal stones that when you look at them you will be happy, and when you touch them you will giggle and wiggle. And I read in the magazine that when you giggle from the crystal touch you will lose your tension and inhibition and you will have a nice vibration. And if you wear a crystal as a necklace and inlay a wide belt with them and wear the belt and never take it off for 6 months, 6 days, 6 hours, and 6 minutes, and when you sleep, spread them upon your bed and under your pillow, you will be able to be a very advanced channel. And you will be able to talk to Cleopatra; Queen of Sheeba; Queen Simeramiese of Babylon; Zubayda, Queen of Baghdad; Robin Hood; Zorro; and the Chief Priest of the Great Pyramid; and Haftasha, the beautiful, charming dancer of Upper Egypt."

And Pum Pum said, "That is very good Num Num."

And Num Num said, "How do you know that you will become spiritual?"

And Puppy Pum Pum said, "I will tell you a few things that bring light to this predicament. When your consciousness becomes clear in situations, your consciousness will warn you against things when they are not proper. And that takes place in the awakening of the "blaming self" -- that if you do something wrong, your conscience will tell you that you are wrong and that you should not do it. Another thing is when inspiration is awake, and that happens in the "inspirational self" when you become creative and innovative and perfect in what you are doing. Another thing is when the "truthful self" becomes alive and you do something, and naturally you know it is right because the truthful self never makes a mistake and that is why it is called the truthful self."

And Num Num said "Ah, that is very nice. I like that. I know that is what I feel now, but I couldn't put it into words."

The Nothing Between Two Nothings

You should know that you come from nothing and you will go to nothing, and in between the two nothings you are nothing. If you don't make something of yourself, and that is the opposite of nothing, then you are nothing. And you may have heard the saying, "He was nothing, but he made something of himself." So why not aim for something worthwhile and do it? Something honorable and good to serve yourself and the world. Something that has a taste of consciousness, spirit, pride and dignity. And God said in the Koran, "There is nothing for a man except what he strives for, and his striving will be fulfilled." But when you are nothing before and nothing after and nothing now, then you are a triple nothing.

That is the situation that plagues human beings. It will be a miracle to find someone who knows what it is all about; to find out if there is something else that exists besides intellect, emotion, senses, technology, the material, lust, greed, selfishness, unhappiness, suffering and tons of negative thoughts that make you like a scarecrow protecting the cabbage and cucumbers. And neither the gopher nor the bluebird pays attention to him. And the raccoon is doing his own entertainment and show by making faces at the scarecrow. And the bluebird in his squeaky voice says to the raccoon, "Encore! Encore! That is the best face-making I've ever seen and I love it." And the scarecrow cannot even scare Kar-Kootch el Moo-Kar-Ketch who lives in the basement beneath the bottom of the sea.

Man Cannot See Beyond His Nose

The negative self holds and dominates the man and keeps him under firm control and in darkness. Man's brain is in a hazy, dazy state, and he trips in a foggy existence, never to see clarity or to know himself except for his name. His mind becomes narrow and he cannot see beyond his nose. And the abundance that is the nature of creation abandons him and casts him out of its generosity. He becomes greedy, selfish, confused, unhappy, phony, and pretentious, and his heart has no feeling, love or imagination. The days keep passing day by day, but he doesn't know the meaning of the day.

And a man has only a certain number of days to live in this life. When they finish, he will be finished. To make the finishing a good finish, he should go to a finishing school to finish the unfinished finish. And he could put a book on his head to learn how to walk with grace or to prance like a beautiful gazelle in a green meadow.

A man without spirit is a finished, polished product of this technical, materialistic progress that is supposed to bring health, wealth, refinement, harmony and peace among men in a Utopian society. And hurray for houses that have doors with five keys that require an orientation class to learn how to lock and unlock these doors to enter inside where hidden treasures of material control the brains of its dwellers. And the roaches pass by mindless of this materiality as if it never existed.

A man without spirit is finished with a finish, and he's finished. His past is finished and his future is finished because he is never in the present. And the present is a magic word, if you know the meaning of it. To know the meaning of it, you need to gather and focus your consciousness, intelligence, being, identity and heart in the creative dynamic existence of the force of *El Khayyum*, which means the sustenance, the expansion and the extension of the inner vitality, intelligence, creativity, spirit, joy, love, life, and the harmony of the moment and its interplay with the existence, the nature, the light, the air, the creation and man.

Man has a little relation to these forces of the moment, just enough to keep him alive. But that relation is exactly like the relation of little children in a little ditch of muddy water, playing -- who, with enthusiastic delight, plunge in the muddy water as if they are in heaven. But these children are unaware of what it would be like to be in warm weather on a tropical island with a sweet clear water pond and a waterfall seeping gently on the rocks, dancing to its natural sound of music and rhythm. And to be impressed by the water in the pond when they meet together like lovers celebrating their meeting after a long separation.

The children in a muddy ditch represent the people in this world. But it's okay for the children because they are children. The children have all the right to be in this ditch of muddy water. God will bless them and make them have more fun.

But the adults in the muddy water of a ditch have no excuse whatsoever to be in that muddy situation. The muddy ditch represents their state in this world. If they don't get out of that mud, they will be dirty and filthy all their lives. And a life with dirt and filth is not worth living. So why don't you clean yourself, be pure and talk to your spirit.

For the adults in a muddy ditch, God might tolerate them for some time; but if they stay in it, the wrath of God will keep them unaware and will cause them to suffer always. They look muddy, dirty, unhappy and have no connection to the dynamic force of the moment. So they complain and suffer with a cylinder in their mouth that puffs smoke and a bottle of wine to dim their intelligence and numb their senses.

To Compete with the Self Is the Pride of Life

If the people were in contact with the dynamic forces that exist in the moment -- and the moment is the guardian of the spirit -- they would be in a state just like that of the tropical island, but better because spirit has no competition. And competition is the way of the ignorant people. Competition makes people greedy, selfish, and hateful towards each other, and destructive. And their hearts turn to solid stone with no feeling, compassion or love. Their goal is to destroy each other, and anger makes them stupid.

But if they have an inner intelligence they would not need to compete against each other, but would compete with their own selves. That is the real competition, that is blessed by the existence and is the pride of life and the way to evolution and fulfillment. It is the real challenge.

And if the people would encounter themselves by challenging themselves, the challenge with other people would melt away and disappear. If they improve themselves, they will be elevated to a higher state of being, awareness and spirit. Passion and love would be the means of communication with other people. They would be helping each other to make life and existence worthy to be called life and existence, with harmony, tranquility and a better purpose in life. And this world would be like a paradise.

35

This world is the gift of the generosity of God. It is only up to the people to understand and appreciate, through awareness, what is at their disposal, and to go ahead and use it with respect, gratitude and thanks. The Koran said, "If you count the blessings of God, you will have no number to contain them." And God said in the Koran also, "He who does good deeds will have contentment and felicity in this life. And he who does bad deeds, his life will be disastrous and suffering."

What is Catalepsy?

Catalepsy is the final abode of materialistic people who live in a world in which the spirit is a commodity that has no market. Catalepsy, as defined in the <u>Random House Dictionary of the English Language</u>, is a physical condition characterized by suspension of sensation, muscular rigidity, fixity of posture, and often by loss of contact with environment.

People without spirit are like graves from which the spirit flew away. And the owl becomes their guardian. But when the spirit is alive, the mind becomes animated. The eyes become shining. The smile becomes magnetic. And the face radiates vigor and lovable energy. And   the body becomes flexible, free of tension, refined and   at ease, when the spirit is alive in it. The spirit is love, peace, contentment and harmony. The spirit is positive energy and purity.

Excess Food Petrifies the Body

When the spirit becomes part of the body, the body will reject all the unfit food that is chemical, processed and artificial. These are the foods that appeal to people who are tense, nervous, negative, confused and without spirit. All that they have is the body. And they constantly have to fill it with food and drinks. If they miss one meal, they panic and they think they are going to die. But the real problem is not missing a meal because they eat all the meals and in between the meals. And even when they eat in between the meals, they dream of meals.

The cow eats all day long without dreaming of a meal. Sometimes the cow sits relaxingly indifferent without tension, worriness, or negative thought, even if there is a hungry lion lurking behind the bushes with his eyes fixed on the cow and his mouth watering is saying to himself, "Oh, boy, what a catch. Won't it be nice to eat that whole cow that could make so many steaks all for myself. But let me wait a little longer to get more hungry."

While the cow is sitting chewing her cud, as if she were sitting on the top of the world, airy and dignified, a little boy, on the other side of the fence, was calling his mother, "Mommy, Mommy! This cow is chewing gum. I am going to go under the fence to the cow and put my hand in her mouth to get some chewing gum."

And the mother said, "No, No! Don't go! You will not like the cow's chewing gum. Here, I have some Wrigley's."

And the boy said, "Ok, but could I go and ride the cow?"

The mother said, "Another time because the movie is going to start and you wanted to see 'Snow White and the Seven Dwarves.'"

And the boy said, "Oh, yeah. I forgot that. But now I remember."

So when people think that they are only body and spend all their lives filling it with food and drink, and they think they live for the body, the body will be heavy, clumsy, tense, stiff, fat, no energy, and weak. And the negative self will chew the spirit like a moth chewing and devouring a Persian carpet. Eating too much food corrupts the body and makes it weak and susceptible to sickness and disease. The mind becomes dull and the face has a doltish look and you fall into an oblivious state. And when you are in that state you never do anything right.

Heedlessness: The Domain of Habit

And that is the forgetful state. It is exactly as if you forget where you put your car keys or any other object and you cannot find it. And in the forgetful state, actually, you forget where you put yourself and you cannot find it regardless of being awake, asleep, talking, walking, laughing, joking, eating, drinking, or smoking. You are in an oblivious state that actually is characterized by habit, condition, ritual, and intellectual knowledge that is only fit for information. The person does not have the direct experience to what is related to the situation.

What makes the matter worse is when you learn about ideas. And you believe the thoughts of other people and you don't even have any connection to them, except emotionally. Belief is a dead conviction when you follow it mechanically without the experience of it. And that stops you from the real learning. When people are in a state of oblivion, they are in a dark state, and they will not understand the secret and the art of how to use food properly and in the right way, to bring about a higher state of awareness, consciousness, evolution, spirit, health, fitness and the joy of life.

Negative Thought is Death

Man is created for a better purpose in life. His purpose is to learn, and not to waste his time in the dark corners of life and existence. People in the dark existence stay in it as long as they live. They are mistaking the relative for the real. The real is heaven. The relative is the outskirts of hellfire. When you are negative, you are experiencing hellfire.

A negative thought carries within it a death power and part of you will die with it, physically, psychically, mentally, emotionally and spiritually. And the more negative thoughts that you have, the more death will encompass you. You will be destroying yourself and it doesn't matter if you think you are alive. The life of an imbecile moron and the life of a gifted genius are not the same but both are living. So, take your choice. You can have negative thoughts that will confuse you or you can have beautiful thoughts that will elevate you.

Beautiful thoughts make your face look like a rose. Negative thoughts make your face look like a mouse in a state of anxiety, tension and fear. You will look like a mouse whose tail has been chewed by a snake as an appetizer to see what it tasted like before eating him.

Roger The Ranger's Hot Dogs

People who are tense, nervous, negative, confused and without spirit have no taste or appreciation and can make no distinction between good food and bad food. You can eat a gourmet shish-kabob that is made by the beautiful Morgana with beautiful, dark, smiling eyes and cheeks that are perfumed with rosewater, who is the girlfriend of Ali Baba of the Mountain of Open Sesame, and who makes the best shish-kabob in Baghdad. Or you can eat a hot dog that is made in a cart on the corner of 42nd Street and 8th Avenue by Roger the Ranger, who chews tobacco all day long and keeps the tobacco in his mouth when he sleeps or otherwise he will have insomnia, and who thinks his hot dogs comes from paradise. He has a sign on the cart which reads, "Hot Dogs from Paradise."

Roger's love affair has always been taking snuff and sneezing all over the hot dogs. He usually doesn't know who he is because of a heavy cocaine addiction. His eyes look red and lifeless with bloated red veins in them that look like a mess of spider webs. And Roger the Ranger is looking at you from behind these spider webs. He looks like a lizard that has been trapped in the spider web.

So Roger the Ranger is one example of many other men in different situations who all suffer from a missing link in their lives. They are the final product of the materialistic, technical and consumer society that boasts of its great developments. This society has many achievements like making plastic roses with which people decorate their chests so they can boost their image and command respect in the eyes of their friends at social gatherings where they enjoy being together to talk, drink coffee, eat donuts and   to savor the taste of wine.

To complete the plight of the spider-eyed man, he wraps himself with colorful Christmas wrapping paper and colored ribbons. And when people see him they will think, "Oh, yes, he is the Spiderman in a disguised appearance, but we know who he is. Let us go and have his hot dogs   and maybe we will be strong like him."

While for the vivacious Morgana, her face radiates with a glow that is warm and gives peace and delight with excitement and living energy. Her smile shines in the heart just like the sun when it appears in a blue sky after a heavy rain of many days with persisting clouds.

Morgana is light like the light and as graceful as a willow tree and gentle and playful as the aspen leaves when they glitter and quiver in the light of the sun. And that is how you feel when you are with Morgana.

Magical Baghdad and the Sunset

On the banks of the Tigris River when the sunset fills the heaven, the river and the earth are the color of glowing warm fire. And at sunset in the beautiful garden of roses in the court of Ali Baba's house that is facing the river, you will find a garden filled with limitless roses.

Baghdad is famed for its roses that make you drunk when you inhale the scent in the air. And roses grow all year round along with other flowers of many different varieties.

And the date trees with their majestic beauty and their golden clusters of succulent dates abundantly hang under the crown of the beautiful leaves with the reflection of the red sunset. They look as if they are dancing pearls in the garden of roses where Morgana and Ali Baba are having their feast. And the meaning of Morgana is pearl.

When the dates are like pearls swaying, they dance with the sunset. And Morgana, the pearl, dances with the dates, the sunset, the quivering aspen and the melodic moment of the willow and the sparkling, gentle waves of the Tigris. This dance of creation led by Morgana, the most fabulous dancer in all of Baghdad, looks like heaven.

Baghdad, because of its splendor and charm, was known as *Sit Al Balad,* which means the mistress of the land. It was the most magical city of its time. That period of history was the Golden Age of life, love, imagination, creativity, evolution, knowledge, spirit, technology and refinement in material; where the material became an object that reflected peace, harmony and joy; and where the material became a mirror to show consciousness flowing like music, to be interwoven with the space around it.

The city's fabulous blue, turquoise, green and golden domes shimmered, glittered and sparkled any time of the day under the bright sun and any time of the night with the moon and stars where Sheherazade reigned on the throne of night and delighted in telling her One Thousand and One Nights Stories of the Arabian Nights.

And the nights of Baghdad are famed for their lush, invigorating breezes that take your breath away to a wonderland while you are in a wonderland, with beautiful palaces, rose gardens and flowing water fountains. Spirit, material and technology become unified in a unity that knows no separation, no limit . . . and there is no other city anywhere to vie with it.

The Power of the Inner Learning in Baghdad

Learning was the sole motive -- finding, discovering, and searching, according to the teaching of Mohammed who said, "Seek knowledge even if it is in China. And seek knowledge from the cradle to the grave." And he said, "Learning is incumbent on the believers -- men and women. And man was created for a higher purpose in life than the triviality of everyday."

So Baghdad became the seat of many marvels and wonders. It was the capital of the civilized world -- wealth and material, spirit and science. Philosophers, scientists, artists, spiritualists, inventors, dancers, musicians and singers all sought Baghdad, which was the mecca of knowledge and learning and which had a highly sophisticated civilization and way of life. It was filled with charming palaces, gardens, bazaars, shows, schools, universities and hospitals which served the public freely.

The splendid mosques were places of learning within the educational system. And the caliphs used to reward translators of books, from other languages to Arabic, with gold to equal the weight of the book. And they gathered all the knowledge, the philosophy, the science, the art and so on from the previous civilizations and other countries. They refined and synthesized all of them. They preserved the worthy knowledge and refuted the chaff, rejecting useless knowledge like rituals, fanatical beliefs, and shallow thinking. They expanded in new dimensions of knowledge and discovery, measuring the circumference of the earth and studying the stars and planets.

And that is why Baghdad was fabulous, because it led the entire known world to a greater way of life and to a great civilization that was based on justice, quality and freedom with great economic development. And the power of spirit was the foundation of all of that. Harmony, peace, and *baraka* (blessing) were the mood of the day and the land.

Beautiful Morgana's Shish-Kabob

That is the environment where beautiful Morgana lived in her rose garden that was filled with the scent of roses on the bank of the river where the date trees were peacefully veiled by the colorful sunset. The trees swayed with the breeze, flooded with the magnificent hues and colors of the sunset in a celebration of joy that filled their surrounding with the love of the living creation.

And the living force of the spirit made its presence felt in the colorful space, in the light, in the shimmering, twinkling and dancing waves ... and in the sun when it is red ... and in the pattern of the rays of the sun as they break through scattered clouds . . . and in the pure roses and the green meadow that is soothingly spread on the side of the river ... and on the smile of Morgana when the exhilarating sunset lights are reflected on her face ... and when the scintillating waves reflect their light like a smile on Morgana's face. And Morgana smiled to the smile of the light and the waves.

And Ali Baba and Morgana sat on colorful pillows savoring and enjoying the shish-kabob. Ali Baba and Morgana talked while watching the charcoal fire and its red color. They enjoyed the water fountain running over black stones that led to a stream down to the Tigris River.

And Morgana turned skewers of onions, green peppers, tomatoes and mushrooms on the charcoal fire. And Ali Baba said, "Oh, Morgana, what a perfect smell of this well done shish-kabob that makes me indulge in eating it and puts me in a state of harmony and relaxation as if I am in heaven. The shish-kabob is so good that even though I am eating, I still feel hungry."

And Morgana said, "Of course, I make the best shish-kabob in Baghdad. Come and sit near me on this comfortable pillow." The pillow rested on a colorful Persian carpet that complemented the color of the roses and gave a feeling of festivity to the garden.

The Dancers of Ali Baba

Ali Baba sat on the pillow and started playing his drum. And Morgana said, "Oh, I love it." She accompanied him on a tambourine and danced lightly. It was a beautiful scene with the color of the sunset creating a magical theatrical light projected from the red heart of the sun. It created a magical environment, creative and fantastic, with the depth of spirit.

When the smile of the roses and Morgana met together with the red and golden scintillation of the quivering and dancing waves of the Tigris River that emulated the dance of Morgana, she sighed and exclaimed, "What a paradise, what a heaven, when heaven comes down to visit Baghdad, *Sit Al Balad.*"

After a little while Morgana put the tambourine aside and brought a large golden tray with another large plate of shish-kabob on it with all the garnishes and freshly baked flat bread that she had just taken from the oven, because Ali Baba could never have enough. While they were eating they heard a knock on the door. Morgana went and opened the door and there were four dancers, friends of Morgana. They greeted each other and she asked them to come to the garden to eat shish-kabob. They said they just finished a dance performance for the Queen of the Turkman who was visiting Baghdad to do some shopping and to enjoy some fabulous gourmet dishes in Baghdad and she loves shish-kabob.

Morgana said, "Come, I've cooked enough shish-kabob for an army. Come and enjoy it."

Samira said, "Oh, yes, I feel famished after all that dancing. But really we ate there and I only said famished because no one can ever say no to Morgana's shish-kabob. I will eat tonight and I will fast tomorrow."

And Sama, Lama and Hana, the other dancers agreed that Morgana's shish-kabob, when you smell it, you get hungry, even if you have eaten all day. So they sat on the pillows enjoying the shish-kabob and the tender bread, fresh, hot and crisp, drinking sweet apricot juice. And for dessert they ate freshly picked juicy dates from the date trees above their heads.

The Crystal Ball and the Wild, Wild West

And Samira brought a crystal ball from her bag saying to Morgana and Ali Baba, "Look what the queen gave me -- a crystal ball! You can tell the future in it by looking in it. And I know Morgana is expert in reading what is in it."

And Morgana said, "Give it to me and let me see." They all sat around her, and she placed the crystal ball on a low table.

And everyone said, "Tell us what you see." And Sama and Lama said, "Tell us of the future of humanity. What will happen to them?"

Morgana looked into the crystal ball and she said, "Oh, I see wonderful things. I am looking in the future and I see a country called America. This particular area that I see is called the Wild, Wild West. They have people there called Red Indians. They wear feathers on their heads. They ride horses without saddles and they eat buffalo but they don't know about shish-kabob. But I imagine they would call it buffalo-kabob but they don't know the word kabob. I see another group there called cowboys and those are cow rustlers. They ride on the back of the wild bull to tame it. And if they don't tame it, the bull will tame them

"I see a man in there. His name is Roger the Ranger and he is very big and very strong. He can carry a cow on his shoulders and do the whirling dervish dance. When he puts the cow down, the cow starts to walk on her head."

Roger The Ranger Jr. Goes to School

"Roger has a ranch and a herd of cows. He is very successful. He has a little boy named Roger, too. He put him in grammar school and the children called him Roger the Ranger. He learned in the school how to fix a fence and how to dig a hole and how to make a coop for the chickens. And he learned some reading and writing but he never learned anything about spirit because nobody seemed to know what spirit was. The school knew nothing of spirit and his family knew nothing of spirit. And the gunslingers who he used to admire and emulate with a wooden gun knew nothing of spirit. In fact, they called the liquor 'spirit'.

"Then he went to college and he learned what he had to learn and became a better football player but he never learned anything about spirit. Life to him seemed so empty and boring. There was no depth in it. He wanted to do something different and meaningful. So he started on marijuana as everyone thought that it was the thing to do to make you relax and feel good. Then he started on cocaine. And in the process he started chewing tobacco. And then he started on heroine.

"He had a job as a bouncer in a club because he wanted to spend more time with the cocaine. He had a few

47

other jobs that did not last because of his habits. Then he decided to leave and go to New York. That is where he settled and started to sell hot dogs on the corner of 42nd Street and 8th Avenue."

When The Hot Dog Has No Spirit

"The material of what the hot dog is made of is refutable and is filled with chemicals and hormones and anyone who eats it will look like a hot dog. But the real problem with the hot dog is that Roger the Ranger has no spirit. And anyone without spirit -- whatever they cook, their food has no blessing and no positive nutrition and never tastes good.

"And Roger the Ranger is one of the whole population that went astray when it came to spirit. They developed their science, technology, material, wealth, economy and got grade A in all these fields; but without spirit, there will be confusion, disturbance, misery and suffering even if everyone was as rich as a billionaire.

"And Roger the Ranger is the product of that highly developed people in technology, material and science who are completely empty of the spirit or even the smell of spirit. And that is the cause of catalepsy and the disintegration from human being to something like a human being but they are not human beings. It is a lost new breed of human being that roams the earth backward and think they are going forward."

And Morgana put the crystal ball aside and said, "This is what I see and it is not too encouraging. Those people will be lost as long as they live. It is better to be with a bird that has spirit and sing from his heart than to be with a man who has no spirit. Men without spirit will eat each other alive."

48

And the three dancers all together said, "Oh, Morgana, let's do some meditative dance before we become like that."

And Morgana said, "Don't worry, you already have beautiful spirits because you learned that since you were children by studying the Koran."

The Spirit Has The Upper Hand

And Morgana said, "Spirit has the upper hand. It is superior to anything that is below it and there is nothing above it. When you become familiar with it you will know that. What drives the spirit away from you is your senses, sensuality, shallow intelligence, negative self and ego.

"Spirit is a pure substance that fills the pure nature. It is the base, the foundation and the living force behind the existence and the depth of existence. The power is in the depth. If the sea has no depth, it will not be a sea. And if man has no depth, he will not be any different from the toys that children play with.

"Any man can acquire spirit and can change from a toy to a complete and perfect man. He can be in perfect harmony with the self, with the world in which he lives and with the existence -- but only if he wakes up from his frivolous, meaningless existence of strife, blankness, isolation and lone-liness.

"And if he doesn't wake up, in the end of his life, he will land in a grave of ignorance and be face to face with darkness, on darkness, on darkness. As long as man is not connected with the spirit, he is no more than a mouse running on a wheel of unlucky fortune that gets him nowhere but to increases his tension and confusion.

"In this technical, materialistic society, man has no concern about other people except as objects of interest to be used for his own purpose to profit from. And this technology, when it is used not in a positive way will cause destruction."

Artificial Food and Artificial People

"A good simple example of that is a commercial poultry farm that uses chemicals and hormones in the food of the chickens and injections to make the chickens fatter and the eggs larger. That chemical will destroy the natural, wholesome taste of the chicken and it will have no taste. And when the meat loses its taste and becomes artificial and people eat it, they will lose their taste and they will have no taste and they will be artificial. Their will blood become chemical and not natural. They will be nervous, tense, confused, rigid, weak, and sick and they will be in a state of catalepsy.

"By eating food filled with chemicals and poison, you will lose your natural behavior as a human being and you become peculiar. And no wonder you see so many people walking the streets who look peculiar and look as if something has been missing in their lives and they wonder what it is. And no wonder you see so many diseases on the rise. The gist of the situation in the long run is slow suicide for millions of people by poisons which are contained in all foods and products. And how long can man live on poison?"

A Machine of Flesh and Bones

When a man is ignorant of his spirit, he becomes a human machine, a machine of flesh and bones. He knows nothing of the intelligence of the heart and its miraculous magic to transform the man to higher levels of knowledge, peace, harmony and learning. He operates only through the intellect of the head that deals with assumption, calculation, figuring, analyzing, emotional expectation, hope, and belief. A belief becomes a dead ritual when it is not based on tests, experience and research of the science of spirit, soul, being, and the dynamic inner strength and power that actually exists in man and that is at his own disposal.

Man's existence is nothing but a sheer opportunity that he should understand, appreciate and respect. If a man wakes up to the real reality while he exists and liberates himself from his frivolousness, his heedlessness, the control of his senses, his negative self and the thoughts of the negative self, then he will experience unity and oneness with the nature and the world. He will be attuned with the invisible world, *El Malaqut*, where he will see a living force and the power of the creation in a dynamic action of sustenance, *El Khayyum*, in the harmony of the eternal living force, *El Hayy*.

People without spirit eat all and everything without limit and without distinction or discrimination. To them, all food is beautiful and equal under the sun. People without spirit see the face of the devil and they think it is an angel. Because when the spirit is absent there is no room for discernment, awareness, understanding and sensitivity. People without spirit operate like a machine more effectively than the real machine. And the real machine has no choice about being a machine. They are made for the purpose of being a machine and nothing more is expected of them.

But human beings who are not made to be machines, make themselves machines by throwing their spirits into the gutter and insisting on and on, on being not only a machine, but a stupid, dumb, human machine. And in doing so, they cut themselves off from anything that is beautiful, delightful, innovative, creative with the zest and vitality that exists in the world and the universe that is everywhere around them.

But when the inner discernment cannot see, then what is there to see but the dark side. And when a human being chooses to be a machine, he will be dark inside and outside. And the miraculous force that is created in the human being disappears. And a human being falls to the lowest of the low. And one of them will sneak through a window, when the occupant is not there, to steal the ironing board with a broken iron. And because the intelligence is not there, he can't figure out that this iron is broken. Not only that, but he steals a frozen head of cabbage. And he takes them to his dwelling and finds that the cabbage had no taste after it has thawed. And that the iron never gets hot.

This is just one example to show you what will happen to human beings when the spirit does not exist. And in a consumer society, theft and stealing always exist.

The Unobtainable Joy of Spirit

People without spirit will never see spirit in each others faces. Ugliness and complaining is a part of their life and they thrive in it. Not in a positive way but in a negative way. They drown in a sea of suffering and disaster and never stop complaining.

The spirit to them is as far as the last planet in the outer galaxy. But the spirit could be as near to them as their nose and as easy to obtain as eating a ripe sweet peach when you are travelling in the Carolinas or Georgia when the peaches are in full bloom. It is also as easy to get the spirit as drinking a glass of orange juice when you are travelling in Florida.

But for ignorant people who do not know the 'how' of making the spirit, they will die without having an inkling of the spirit. People without spirit tend to be skeptical. The absence of the spirit causes a limitation in the understanding and obliterates the discernment of the heart. And the intellect goes mish-mash, analyzes, and judges without fact or experience.

Sweet Conversation is the Essence of Life

The dirt has no spirit and when people have no spirit then they are equal to dirt. And when the wind comes by, the dirt will be dust. And when the rain comes by, the dirt will be mud. And in between the dust and the mud, there is no space for innovation, creation, imagination, and sweet conversation.

Sweet conversation is the asset and essence of life. And life is beautiful, tender and charming with sweet conversation. And God said in the Koran, "Sweet words rise to heaven and come back with blessing."

Spirit makes people gentle and noble, and their behavior pleasant and timely. When there is no spirit, the lives of the people will be heavy, and they rely on their senses and sensual pleasure. And their life becomes like a cold, dreary, foggy, bleary gray mist in a swamp that is infested by alligators -- dark and cold. And they are wading in the swamp to get out of it but they settle for hot apple pie and vanilla ice cream and coffee in a coffee shop to bring pleasure and to impose happiness by working their teeth in the hot apple pie and cold vanilla ice cream. And they exclaim, "How delicious! I love it! And I could eat it all day long!"

When the World Is a Perfumed Rose

Life is beautiful like a perfumed rose, when the spirit is awake and alive. And the moment feels the life in the spirit and moves gently towards it, like a sailboat sailing   to the heart of the red sun when the sun comes down from the heaven and embraces the gentle and colorful waves on the horizon. And the sun kisses the sea and the face of the sea becomes crimson and warm.

And the sea says to the sun, "I was waiting for you all day to come down from heaven to feel the warmth of your alluring and lovable nearness that sends warmth to my heart. And you make me dance when you throw on me a colorful garment that is woven of magical radiant beams of elegant color and splendor, fair, tender, soft, rich, and graceful. I love it! I live it! I breathe it! And I am mesmerized by it. And there is nowhere in the entire world, nowhere, where I would like to be but with you."

And the moment feels the life in the spirit and gravitates tenderly to the spirit. And the moment says to the spirit, "I bring to you the breath of the perfumed rose." The perfumed rose is the world and life when the spirit awakens to it.

The spirit is pure. The spirit is light. Purity and light attract each other. There is light in purity and purity in light. Both create a presence of peace, tranquility, joy and a dazzling sensation and manifestation beyond the limit of intellect, senses, imagination and reasoning.

The veil of the invisible world will be lifted and you will be face to face with a reality that every moment of it is peace, love, felicity, creativity, and a sea of spirit. And like a drop of water your spirit will go to the sea of spirit and the sea will come to you and you will become a sea of spirit.

It is only when you have purity and light that it will be possible to experience the invisible world through spiritual insight and mystical vision.

People of the Mirage

and

Other Stories

People of the Mirage

When you are thirsty, there is nothing in the entire world to quench your thirst better than water. Water is the ultimate and best drink for thirst. You could have all kinds of juices and drinks, cool and perfect, but the water is the real thing for the thirst and no other things do the same.

For a man in a desert who is very thirsty and sees the mirage far away, it looks like water. And he runs after it and it runs away. And the thirst creates an anxiety to keep him running and not able to think. And the thirst eventually will kill him before finding the water.

When people have no spirit, they will be in the same situation as the thirsty man in the desert who ran after the mirage, mistaking it for water. People will run left and right to find happiness and pleasure, looking always for the same thing. But the real thing that they are looking for is inside of them and they don't know it. So it is missing or lost in a maze of ignorance and useless confrontation with their minds, senses, desires and lust that nothing could satisfy, not even the whole of the universe. They want to fill what is missing from the outside to feel complete or perfect.

But the complete and perfect things that they are looking for will never be complete or perfect because they are looking for it in the wrong place and they are trapped in a deep, dark, black hollow of hunger, despair and anxiety within themselves. And the spirit can't be found anywhere whether inside or outside. The spirit is like a mystery lost in a black mist in a maze of dark night where the sun never rises and the light is never known.

The spirit is there within you. And because it is there, it can be found. It is only when things do not exist that they cannot be found.

When the people live without spirit they will be like puppets that move with strings and laugh at each other. And their lives are nothing but a trivial matter in a matrix of frivolity. And that happens when the spirit is lost.

And the spirit is lost when people are born into a society that knows nothing of the practical spirituality, except that they know the word spirit and use it at random as a word only, without knowing the meaning or the depth of the spirit. And actually they are in a hazy, shaky state as far as the spirit is concerned. The spirit to them is like a glass of water without the water. And a glass without water is an empty glass. And a body without spirit is an empty body.

So when children are born into a society that is divest of spirit that means they are divest of the real love and the real humanity. When there is no spirit, people will be like a mannequin with a motor. You turn it on and they move, dance, talk, smile. But the spirit is not there. It is a dead reality that brings nothing but death, and propagates death and living in a state of death. And it glorifies their achievement and progress as a great civilization: The Civilization of the Mannequin with a Motor.

Babies born in this great civilization have parents that know nothing of the spirit. So the parents take care of the body of the child and the spirit is turned loose like a wild goose and runs away like a lost puppy.

And the child grows up in a twisted way of existence through conditioning and habits. He falls in a pattern of forms that have no essence, and becomes enslaved to the habits. And the habits, little by little, create of the child a weak creature, and lower his capacity and understanding. And the man functions in the society as everyone does, with complete ignorance of who he is. He is not in a wakeful state.

The wakeful state operates with a natural inner rhythm that coincides with the rhythm of the environment and surrounding, and an inner awareness and discernment that is part of the awareness of the existence, and an innate intelligence of the living force of the cosmos that is focused in the heart and not the intellect of the head.

Wrong doing and mistakes do not exist in a wakeful state. Wrong doing and mistakes exist only in the state of forgetfulness. Sorrow and suffering are the companions of the forgetful state that is also the ignorant state that is the lowest and worst state that a man could get in. It is not natural or real. It is not perfect or good.

But when man doesn't know the real, he thinks the unreal is real. And a madman in a mental hospital will think he is the wisest man. And a man in a bar will drink a gallon of whiskey and then stand on a table and with a loud voice will say, "I am as pure as a maiden red rose blossoming in springtime with the refreshing breeze and the warm, gentle light of the sun." And then he will lay down on the table and sleep.

A prancing gazelle in a green meadow is unlike a fat elephant who goes to Weight Watchers and tries to prance like a gazelle. And that is what the people without spirit look like: fat elephants who want to prance like a gazelle and believe it. And when they see a real gazelle in a green meadow dancing, bouncing, leaping in the air, then their belief will shatter to pieces. Maybe by then they will do something to transform

61

themselves into something worthwhile.

A man is given intelligence that is good enough. If he uses it right he will hold the heaven between his hands. If a man looks to heaven, he will have heaven and earth. But, if he looks to the earth, he will lose heaven and earth. But man always chooses all and everything that will cause him to suffer and live in a thorny mental state.

A man in the forgetful state or ignorant state will be extremely happy to have a dinner in a dimly lit restaurant with a candle in front of him. And his thought will be absorbed with affinity to the flame of the candle. A man will do so because he has lost connection to the real light, the light of heaven that pours in the heart. The word for heart in Arabic is *khalb*.

One of the meanings of *khalb* is continuous change, moment to moment, in an evolutionary way to a higher meaning and purpose in life through enlightenment. And when the heart is open to the light of heaven, the heart becomes the light of heaven. And the wakeful state is the product of that. And a man will be exposed to a thousand inner suns. And no flickering candle flame is necessary when you are with a thousand suns.

People without spirit are displaced from the pleasure of the harmony of the beautiful reality. They are in the center of it but they can't see it -- the pleasure of the light of the sun and the splendid calm moon playing hide and seek with the glowing, flowing clouds dancing brilliantly in the light of moon with a peaceful smile; and the moon tenderly sailing among them casting joyous light to their smiles; and the smile becomes tender spirit flowing in the liquid moonlight and harmony that fills the space, the gentle breath, the soft breeze that fills the heart with life.

When there is no spirit, it is like someone who lost his brain or has no brain, who peels an orange and eats the peel and looks directly at the peeled orange and can't figure out what it is. And when the spirit is not there, people try to find it in a dress, in a suit, in a shirt, in shoes, in a ring, in a necklace, in a scarf, in lipstick, perfume, teddy bears and plastic apples. And because they cannot find it in these objects, they will go again and again to big department stores and malls, that have become a way of life, or on a safari hunt.

And all of the catch that they caught in their safari excursion, or you could say, all the junk that is displayed immaculately with lights, perfume, and music that captures the hearts and the minds of the hunters in this safari hunt, in elevators and on escalators, on the balcony, in an alcove, in an arbor, in a basement, in a hall of fame of Who Wears What of the latest fashions and designs from the famous houses like Tortino Meetano Chorciani of Rome, and Francois Souffle Wass Wass of France and Chin Chin Cho Lo Cho Lo of Hong Kong and Tojo Motochuchi of Japan.

And these safari hunters feel happy, exhilarated, as if they are in heaven, buying and hoarding all of these objects and carrying the packages quickly to the food concession area to complete the pleasure of buying with the pleasure of eating.

When they finish their shopping, as if they were hunting lions and tigers and snakes 25 feet long, they order hot dogs and hamburgers and enjoy their outing. Then they go home and their heart goes in gloom and their mind sinks in depression. Then another day, they are ready again for the safari hunt to uplift the heart.

They keep repeating this uplifting again and again, but they never quench their thirst to find the spirit in the mirage of material that was dead to start with and that is dead now and will be dead later.

And you never find spirit when dealing with something that is dead. You only acquire more attributes of death to be part of your personality and to be a man neither alive or dead. And when you are neither alive nor dead, your life is nothing but misery: empty, hollow, shallow, tense and negative.

And you ask the computer, "Who am I?" And the computer will tell you, "You are nothing but a creature of *Ahdam*." The meaning of *Ahdam* is nonexistent. As long as you have no spirit, whatever you do or accomplish in this world has no value or importance. And when you go, they will go.

The only value that there is, is in the spirit.

When You Are a Stranger to Yourself

If you want to be something of value, you have to get rid of anything that stands in the way between you and your spirit. For whatever stands between you and your spirit is like a thick, iron wall. You will be on one side and your spirit will be on the other side. You will be a stranger to your spirit. And when you are a stranger to your spirit, you will be a stranger to yourself. You will lose contact with the reality and to the source of living energy, to the ease of the vital flow and to the subtle, gentle energy of harmony that exists in the space. But it is hidden and protected from those who are heedless and strangers to themselves. And when they can't find that living energy that gives harmony and peace -- and peace is the food of the spirit, then the spirit has no food and it will die, just like a bird in a cage when you don't give him food.

To be without spirit is an exaction and a destruction of the true character of a human being. A life without spirit is a turbulent and exasperating everyday experience. And a man is more apt to be called a beastman than a gentleman.

When many men become beast-like, then you will have a beastly society: unmindful, unconcerned for each other, selfish, greedy, suspicious and doubtful. And they will cram rules, ordinances, regulations and laws abundantly and without reservation, just like when you cram books for the final exam. They do all of that to straighten their lives but their lives are never straight. And the proof of that is unlimited rules and laws. And that is a sign of a big twist and crookedness that even a crocodile would feel hinged to his liberty and freedom.

With more rules, ordinances, and laws, they create

more problems and confusion. And then they have to make more rules, ordinances, and laws. And then they have more problems and confusion. And then they need to make more rules, ordinances and laws. And on and on and on.

Progressive, educated people need rules and laws to straighten their lives and give them a lift and to boost their image as civilized people: $1000 fine for littering the highway; and $500 fine for spitting in the hallway.

A man is driving on the highway going home around six o'clock in the evening when the highway is packed with cars, fender to fender, and he has already spent two hours driving like a snail. Then he sees a little opening in the highway and he feels a respite and goes a little faster than the snail speed. And in a hidden corner under a bridge, like an alcove, a highway patrol car is hiding like a shark, hungry to catch a fish. He turns on his red light and pushes on the accelerator to quickly encompass the man who is driving a little faster than the snail speed. He gives him a ticket saying, "I am sorry... you broke the rule."

If the patrolman and the man who drove a little faster than the snail speed, the city hall and whoever put these rules, ordinances and laws together had common sense, discernment, awareness, perception, intuition and love of humanity, the situation would be completely different.

But these subjects are unknown and are not taught in the schools. They are blank and none of these can be seen on the computer. And that is the cause of the mumble, jumble fuzzy logic. So do the mambo dance and eat gumbo and wait for fuzzy logic in the computer science that is coming from Japan to find rules and laws neither wrong nor right. And when you are fuzzy, nothing really counts.

Complaining, unhappiness, and being negative and angry are the result of not having equilibrium. To be negative and angry is the worst affliction that a human being can have. It is the most abominable, loathsome, abhorrent, detestable state that a man can be in. It keeps the man dumb and stupid. It robs him of his peace and harmony and keeps him insensitive. It ruptures the mechanical function of the intellect. It destroys the in-telligence of the heart and shatters the affection and love and replaces them with scorn and hate.

If a man ponders on the cause of his anger and finds out what it is and tries to solve that problem by avoiding the cause of the anger, then he will be wise, gentle, lovable, sensitive and pleasant to be with. But if he doesn't learn how to destroy the cause of the anger, then the anger will destroy him. He will look like a mouse that had been bitten by one hundred scorpions. He will be dull, brainless, unpleasant, harsh, unsuitable for conversation and repugnant and his negative energy will radiate and fill one square mile around him.

If you get in the radius of it, you will have stomach cramps and you will be nauseated and vomiting. And you will think that the world is turned upside down. An earthquake will be much more fun to be in than to be in the vicinity or near an angry, negative, complaining man.

To avoid being in a situation with a negative person and his complaining, run away and never look back or the negative vibration will clutch at your neck. Run away to an open space with the fresh air and say, "Thank you God for giving me the strength to run away." And in the open space, you can rejoice and breathe.

And for the angry, negative man who alienated his spirit because spirit never comes near a complaining, negative, angry person, his life is always a disaster and punishment is inflicted on him by his own ignorance.

There is a gentle energy of harmony that exists in the space but it is hidden and protected from those who are heedless, negative and angry. The spirit abandons them and they are lost wherever they are. They will have a puzzled phony look on their faces and they are counterfeit human beings and not real.

They walk as if they own the world and as if the world owes them a million dollars. Arrogant, with their heads in the air and their faces with a rigid, plastic expression, floating and swaggering on the ground, to give the impression of importance. But it is a fact that arrogance is a sign of emptiness, ignorance and stubbornness that many people misunderstand.

When people have no spirit, they have no contact with each other or the environment or the surroundings or even with a chair. And whether the chair is for sitting or standing, it is all the same. They see the form but not the depth that exists in any object.

That depth in any object will be felt, if you have a depth within you. And when the depth of the man connects with the depth of an object, the object will manifest an energy that is stillness in action. You feel relaxation, ease and harmonious communication with the object. And you feel a connection with the object. And you feel a connection that brings you strength, energy and vitality that works as a powerful healing and purification. And the spirit will fill the space around you as far as your eyes can see.

The Essence Is the Real Pleasure

When there is a balance between the mundane and the spirit, between the outer and the inner, life becomes more appropriate to be called life. It will be charming, easy, pleasant and going in the right direction without complication or tension.

When you do work that you enjoy, actually, you are doing a service to yourself, to the people, and to humanity. The work that you enjoy will develop your capacity for learning in a practical way and it will make you an ideal person. It will lead you to understand perfection and perfection creates a connection to the real and to the truth.

To do a work with joy and contentment will lead you to your essence. And when you are in the essence, you will see the essence in the world. And essence talks to essence. And essence smiles to essence. And if the rose has no essence, nobody will know the perfume. When your essence bubbles with life, you become a living human being, instead of a wishy-washy human being.

You will be a real-life cowboy, instead of a drug store cowboy. You will be attractive and bright like the light of the sun instead of being like a flickering candle in a dark, dingy, smoky, basement bar with a lot of trash barrels with a stinking smell as if they are standing there at the door as a replacement for the host, as a welcome to the people.

People with essence gravitate toward elegant, plush places. People with no essence gravitate toward the above mentioned dark, dingy, smoky basement bar. People with no essence are deprived of sensitivity. People with essence, their sensitivity vibrates like an electric current and shimmers like the sun when the sun dances to the rainbow. People without essence are devoid of taste whether on the tongue or in the mind. People with essence have a taste that transforms them to ecstasy and delight.

To do work that gives you contentment and joy will make you straight, erect and pliable in your mind. And the essence is your usher. To do work that you dislike, you will be bowed, twisted and stiff with a distorted mentality and a pinch in your nervous system. Your life will be dark and your day negative. And your dreams will be negative.

The Arabic word for negative is *sah lib*. Besides meaning negative, the other meaning of *sah lib* is to deplete the mind of anything that is positive and also to deprive the person materially, spiritually and psychologically. Also it means ineffective, blank and useless. Another meaning of *sah lib* is the highway robber who will take everything from you and leave you with nothing.

So the word "negative" is destructive. It destroys the mind. And its effect continues on to ruin all the faculties and slowly destroy the body. Weakness and sickness become permanent companions. The body will be ugly, unbalanced, clumsy, rigid, inflexible, dour and petrified, and catalepsy will be your dwelling.

Dinner with God

To exist in this world is the greatest opportunity that ever came your way or made your way possible. And you try to hold and seize that opportunity, and respect and value it and look up to it and use it positively -- to whatever it might take you to find, to explore, to discover, to understand -- to unfold what is hidden, to open what is closed, and to approach the invisible world. And to be able to do that, you need to exist. And that existence has to be excellent and to be positive and never negative.

Negative ways and moods destroy the ease and tranquil state. It blocks the natural receptivity of the mind and the heart. Receptivity is a natural gentle state. It takes place between the intuitive heart and the easy thoughts of the mind. Its nature is sweet and tender. Its main action is to be open to creative and innovative vibration that comes from the cosmic intelligence or that is received from positive people or beautiful creatures.

To have the body and to live with your mind, your heart, and all the rest of you, is the most valuable thing that you have in this existence. So take care of it and use it positively to the best of your knowledge. Do not waste a minute, by letting yourself decline. Be awake and never let yourself slumber because that is the time when the negative self opens itself to the dark forces and they will creep all over you, unnoticeably, until it is too late to notice.

All the conditioning, habits, weakness and addictions will bring destruction and take away all the good things within you and throw them down the gutter. And weakness will take the place of the good things.

71

This will only happen when you are in a heedless state. So shake that state and be awake and shout like Tarzan to scare the cigarette, the coffee, the chocolate, the donuts, the coke, the cake, the wine, the liquor, the cocaine, the heroin and the crack before it cracks your brain.

Be strong, free, gentle, helpful and noble. And God will have dinner with you even though God doesn't eat. But he will make an exception just to sit with you. And God will entertain you in a way that all other entertainments on earth fade away as if they have never been.

This world is the beginning, the start and the expansion to a thing that is greater than what you see. There are higher things that exist. You have to look for it and grow within it. Otherwise, you will stay throughout your life in this world as a child in kindergarten entangled with toys, games and wooden blocks to build houses for little plastic goats. And you will be the shepherd. It makes no difference whether they will be goats or sheep.

Harmony with the Self

If you have a car and the wheels are not balanced, and then you drive it on the highway, it will start to shake. And you will shake with it. And you could sing, "Shake, Baby, Shake." If you have a man and he is not balanced and something goes wrong, he will shake too. So the balance is very important whether in a car or a man.

When you are balanced, it means that all the forces and faculties within you are in harmony. And when your balance is harmonious, you will see the life around you as an object of harmony even though other people around you are not in harmony. But that does not matter because you are in harmony with yourself. And if all the things outside yourself are not in harmony, you will still be in harmony. The inner harmony is the most important and it is what counts. And when you have the harmony and another person does not have it, this will give you a measurement to see where you are as compared to the person who is afflicted by misery and confusion.

The only reason that person is afflicted with misery and confusion is because he is greedy, selfish, unhelpful and self-centered. When a person has these traits God will make him miserable and cause him to suffer. And God does not like people who are greedy, selfish, unhelpful and self-centered.

The more the person is greedy and selfish, the curse is his misery and confusion. And no one who is selfish and greedy in this world will escape the consequences of his own stupidity. And firmly he establishes his own punishment by the fear that fills his heart.

And his mind will be like a puzzle whose pieces came

from different puzzles. And none of these pieces will fit together. And the puzzle will never achieve anything more than a puzzle.

And this is how the mind is for people whose lives are nothing but a puzzle. And their faces look like a puzzle but the pieces never fit together.

And God will bless a happy dog with a face so soft and tender that he makes you smile because he is never negative or confused, more than a man with a sullen face, snobbish, snarling and harsh, who wakes up complaining and goes to bed complaining.

For further information about Adnan's summer
program and touring schedule, contact:

Sufi Foundation of America
P.O. Box 170
Torreon, NM 87061
Phone: (505) 384-5135
Website: www.SufiFoundation.org

www.ingramcontent.com/pod-product-compliance
Lightning Source LLC
Chambersburg PA
CBHW021219020426
42331CB00003B/376